W9-BWS-777

Rosie the Riveter: Women in a Time of War

Rosie the Riveter

Women in a Time of War

Developmental Studies Center • Oakland, California

Copyright © 2008 by Developmental Studies Center

All rights reserved. Except where otherwise noted, no part of this publication may be reproduced in whole or in part, or stored in a retrieval system, or transmitted in any form or by any means, electronic, mechanical, photocopying, recording, or otherwise, without the written permission of the publisher. For information regarding permissions, write to the Editorial Department at Developmental Studies Center.

First edition published 2008.

Photographs and images: Getty Images, Inc. Copyright © 1999–2008 Getty Images, Inc. All rights reserved. (cover); Corbis Corporation. Copyright © 2001–2008 by Corbis Corporation. All visual media © by Corbis Corporation and/or its media providers. All rights reserved. (pp. ii, vi, 2, 3, 5, 7, 8, 11, 15, 16, 17, 19, 21); Library of Congress, www.loc.gov (pp. 4, 5, 9, 17).

Developmental Studies Center
2000 Embarcadero, Suite 305
Oakland, CA 94606-5300
(800) 666-7270, fax: (510) 464-3670
www.devstu.org

ISBN-13: 978-1-59892-760-3
ISBN-10: 1-59892-760-4

Printed in Mexico
2 3 4 5 6 7 8 9 10 RRD 17 16 15 14 13 12 11 10 09

CONTENTS

> "It wasn't expected of me to go to work or my sister to go to work. We did because the war was on."
>
> — Marian Sousa, draftsperson during World War II

INTRODUCTION

The outbreak of World War II brought dramatic changes for women in the United States. Up until that time, most people believed that women should stay home and take care of their families and households. Most employers did not hire women to do jobs traditionally held by men. For the most part, jobs outside the home that were available to women were jobs men didn't want. When the United States entered World War II, women in the U.S. found themselves suddenly being asked to play a vital part in the war effort. Every day they were proving themselves as capable as men in the workforce. They were developing new skills and new ideas about themselves and the world, and, in doing so, creating changes that we still feel today.

War had been raging worldwide since 1939. Japan was fighting to conquer other countries in Asia. Germany, led by Adolf Hitler, was invading its neighbors and attempting to build an empire in Europe. Until 1941, the U.S. government had managed to stay out of the conflict, and the lives of most Americans weren't much affected by the war. But all of that changed on the morning of December 7, 1941.

At 8 a.m. on that clear Sunday morning, a wave of Japanese bombers and fighter planes swept over the U.S. naval base at Pearl Harbor in Hawaii, launching a devastating attack on American ships and military airfields. An hour later, a second wave of planes brought more destruction. By the end of the day, the U.S. naval force was crippled. Twenty-one ships and 188 planes were destroyed or damaged, and more than 2,400 people, including **civilians**, were killed.

The surprise attack stunned the nation. On December 8, 1941, the U.S. officially entered World War II when President Roosevelt signed a declaration of war against Japan.

Headlines from **The New York Times** the day after the Pearl Harbor attack

President Roosevelt signs the declaration of war against Japan.

"There is one front and one battle where everyone in the United States—every man, woman, and child—is in action. …That front is right here at home, in our daily lives."

— President Franklin D. Roosevelt

[From *The Public Papers and Addresses of Franklin D. Roosevelt*, Harper & Brothers, 1941]

ASIA AND EUROPE

Because of an agreement Germany and Italy had with Japan, those two countries declared war on the U.S. two days later. Now the U.S. would have to fight on battlefronts in Asia and Europe, thousands of miles apart. Having to divide the military between these two **theaters of war** led to a serious shortage of troops. Millions of men rushed to sign up for military service, and new **recruits** were in constant demand.

With thousands of their fathers, sons, brothers, and husbands leaving daily to join the conflict, Americans left at home could no longer view the war as a distant event happening overseas. It would affect not only the troops, but American citizens at home, going about their daily lives.

NEEDS ON THE HOME FRONT

To fight two wars at the same time, the U.S. needed to manufacture thousands of new planes, ships, tanks, and guns, all in a short period of time. New factories had to be built and existing ones made bigger. For Americans on the **home front**, addressing the U.S. military's severe shortage of equipment was one of the most important parts of the war effort.

Huge amounts of raw materials such as steel and coal were needed to produce this new **arsenal**. Nationwide salvage drives were held to collect tin cans, scrap metal, glass bottles, and rubber because these materials could be recycled and used to manufacture military equipment. Materials such as nylon and silk could be used to make parachutes, and cooking fat could be recycled and used to make explosives. Women did much of the work that made the salvage drives successful.

Material collected from a salvage drive

Left: Victory gardeners show off their vegetables.
Right: A woman buys rationed goods in a New York City grocery store.

MAKING DO WITH LESS

Because of the need to provide millions of soldiers in Europe and Asia with food and supplies, the U.S. government introduced **rationing** for Americans at home. Families were issued ration cards, allowing them to buy only small amounts of certain goods, such as coffee, sugar, meat, and shoes, in order to ensure an adequate supply for troops overseas. The government urged people to start their own vegetable gardens—called "victory gardens"—to grow food for themselves. Bicycling was encouraged over driving to save fuel.

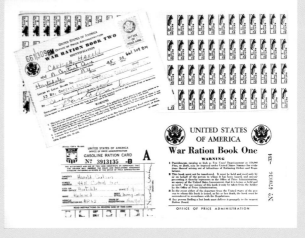

Ration cards

Some items weren't available at all. Altha Humphrey, who was a young girl during the war years, remembers:

> "There were no silk stockings for the ladies to wear, so my mother used to use makeup on her legs to make them look just a little bit tanned. Then they took a pencil, I guess like an eyebrow pencil, and they put a line up the backs of their legs so they could look like they had stockings on...."

With men either away at work or fighting overseas, women had full responsibility for running their households and keeping their families fed and clothed, all while "making do with less."

WOMEN AS VOLUNTEERS

Women were asked to do unpaid work outside the home to support the troops. Women volunteered for organizations such as the Red Cross and the Women's Voluntary Service. They knitted and sewed clothes and rolled bandages for soldiers on the battlefront. They learned first aid to help in emergencies. Some women were trained to drive trucks to **evacuate** people to safety in case of an invasion.

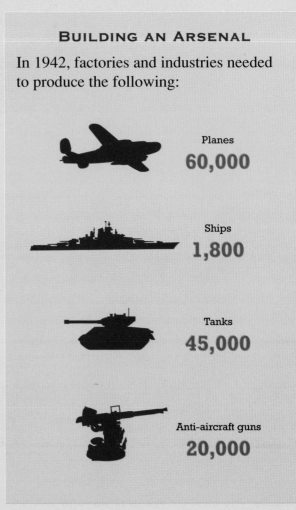

BUILDING AN ARSENAL

In 1942, factories and industries needed to produce the following:

Planes
60,000

Ships
1,800

Tanks
45,000

Anti-aircraft guns
20,000

Top: Members of the Women's Voluntary Service roll bandages.
Bottom: Young women in Kentucky knit clothes for soldiers during the war.

Though women were doing their part on the home front, it soon became clear that they would have to do even more to support the war effort. Millions of men were leaving their jobs to join the war, which created a severe shortage of workers at home. The only way that the U.S. could produce enough military equipment to win the war was to welcome women into the paid workforce, offering them jobs that had been considered, until that point, "men's work."

PROPAGANDA: WOMEN CAN DO IT!

To attract women into the workforce, the government launched a **propaganda** campaign directed at them. The campaign was organized

by the Office of War Information (OWI), a government agency created to keep people informed about the progress of the war. The OWI created propaganda posters and helped magazines and newspapers come up with ideas for articles and advertisements that would encourage women to go to work.

War propaganda directed toward women included slogans such as, "Women in the War: We Can't Win Without Them" and "Count on Us! We Won't

Let You Down!" These slogans were designed to appeal to women's love of country and sense of duty. They suggested that without women's efforts, the lives of their loved ones would be in danger. As a result, millions of American women entered the workforce.

Women went to work in factories, offices, and stores. At least 6 million women entered the workforce for the very first time. As women went to work, they began to feel a sense of pride to be working for their country and supporting the soldiers on the battlefront. Many found that they enjoyed working with other people toward a common goal. Patricia Buls, a draftsperson in the shipyards, explains:

> *"I think most everybody who worked there felt that there was a job that had to be done. I mean, there was a war to be won, and everybody had a job to do to help win that war...."*

PROPAGANDA

Propaganda is the spreading of ideas or information to further a cause or change people's opinions or behavior. Although propaganda can be true, information is often **distorted** or exaggerated in order to get a message across.

"WE DON'T TAKE WOMEN OR BLACKS"

Even though women were desperately needed in the workforce and many women were willing to work, they still faced **discrimination**. Some employers wouldn't hire married women if men or single women were available. Others refused to hire women at all, even if they were short of workers.

Some male workers refused to work alongside women. When the labor shortage forced the Kelsey Hayes Wheel Company in Detroit to hire women, the men in the company went on **strike**. As a result of the strike, the company was forced to limit the number of women it hired and keep them out of skilled jobs.

Phyllis Gould, who became a welder, recalls trying to get a job, which required that she first join a **union**:

"So I went to the union hall, and my memory of that place is all dark. [laughing] It was a dark place, and [there was] this big man that was dressed in dark clothes and he just said, 'No. We don't take women or blacks.' Only that's not the word he used. So I went home. And the next day, I went again, same routine. The third day I didn't go to the [union] hall. I went up to the window at the hiring hall, and they said, 'No,' and I started to cry. As I'm walking back through this room there was a man at a desk and he said, 'What's wrong?' and I told him. I don't know what he did but he says, 'Go back up there.' And I did, and they gave me the job. . . . Then they hired five or six more women and a chaperone, because we were the first."

ROSIE THE RIVETER

The most successful piece of propaganda included a character known as Rosie the Riveter. She first appeared on a poster with the slogan "We Can Do It!" in 1942 and became a symbol of all American working women in World War II. The following year, Rosie was featured on the front page of *The Saturday Evening Post* newspaper. A song about Rosie was released in early 1943.

The "We Can Do It!" poster encouraged American women to work to support the war effort.

Rosie the Riveter was inspired by a real-life **riveter**. Her name was Rose Will Monroe. She was born in Kentucky in 1920. During the war, Monroe moved to Michigan with her two children in search of work. She got a job building bombers for the air force at an aircraft factory. She was working at the factory when she was asked to appear in a film **promoting** the war effort.

Monroe was described by her daughter as someone who could do everything. During the war, she wanted to learn to fly but she wasn't allowed to because she was a single mother. When she was in her 50s, she got her pilot's license. After the war, Monroe kept on working: She was a taxi driver, ran a beauty store, and started up a building company. She died in 1997 at the age of 77.

As the war continued and more and more working men left their jobs to join the military, employers had to change their ideas about what was "acceptable" work for women. This meant more and better job opportunities for women entering the workforce.

NEW JOBS, NEW SKILLS

Women drove trucks and taxis, operated cranes, loaded and tested machine guns, and helped build planes and tanks. War propaganda helped convince women they could do skilled factory jobs by building on skills they already used in their household work.

Employers who had resisted hiring women for skilled jobs were forced to reconsider. Phyllis Gould describes a **supervisor** who at first assigned the more interesting, challenging jobs only to men:

> *"Every step he took I was in lockstep with him, and every time he'd point to that and start to tell some guy to do it, I'd say, 'I can do it.' And finally, he just said, 'Well, do it!' He didn't think I could, but I could. So that was the first step in really asserting myself...."*

Changing attitudes combined with a growing need for workers led employers to hire women for some of the most skilled jobs in factories and production plants—working as **welders**, carpenters, electricians, and mechanics.

Some women who had started in unskilled jobs were able to get promoted to better-paying jobs through hard work and **perseverance**. Mary Newson, for example, migrated from the rural South to California and began working at an automobile assembly plant as a janitor. Eventually, she was promoted to working on the assembly line, making floorboards for cars. Over time, she became an inspector in charge of quality control.

Slowly but surely, public opinion about "women's" and "men's" work began to shift. By 1942, the number of jobs seen as suitable for women had increased dramatically.

BRINGING HOME A PAYCHECK

It was not only a sense of duty to country that led many women to seek out war work. The promise of a brighter financial future caused women, especially **impoverished** women from the rural South and Midwest, to move to areas that were centers for military-related industry, such as Richmond, California.

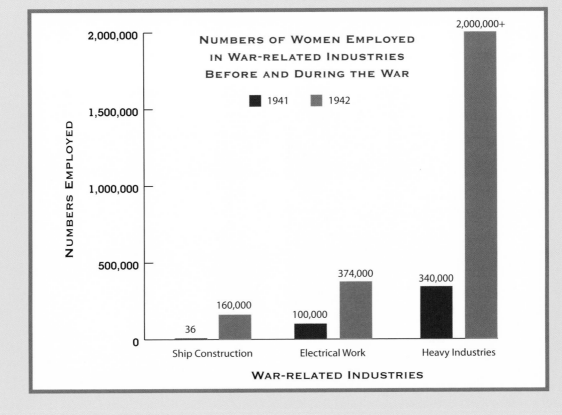

NUMBERS OF WOMEN EMPLOYED
IN WAR-RELATED INDUSTRIES
BEFORE AND DURING THE WAR

■ 1941   ■ 1942

Numbers Employed vs. *War-related Industries*

- Ship Construction: 36 (1941), 160,000 (1942)
- Electrical Work: 100,000 (1941), 374,000 (1942)
- Heavy Industries: 340,000 (1941), 2,000,000+ (1942)

For many working women, earning their own money was a new and exhilarating experience.

For the first time in their lives, they didn't need to depend on others for financial security. Harriete Stewart, who worked as a nurse in the shipyards, describes getting her first paycheck:

"I remember looking at that paycheck and rubbing it, and rubbing it, and folding it, and putting it away, and taking it out and looking at it again." [laughter]

Although war work gave women new ways to earn a living, most women still received lower pay than men doing the same work. In 1944, the average weekly wage for men working in a war-related industry was $54.65, while for women it was $31.21. Still, these wages felt reasonable to women compared to what they earned in the low-paying jobs available to them before the war.

NEW CONFIDENCE

In addition to the satisfaction of earning their own money, the skilled factory and production jobs brought women a deep sense of pride in their work. They discovered interests, talents, and abilities they didn't know they had. They felt **competent** and independent in a way they never had before. Phyllis Gould recalls:

> *"I was a good welder and I loved it. It was so satisfying. I had always done embroidery, and you want your stitches all to [be] even and look nice. Well, it was the same with welding. As you overlapped each pass you wanted them to be the same—the spacing—and to look nice and be good, too. So eventually I became, I guess, a prima donna on the crew, and I got to do pretty much what I wanted to do."*

Another welder, Polly Russell, also describes her positive feelings about her work:

> *"Now I think back, I says, 'How did I do it?' Evidently I was young and capable…. I used to be very proud of my welds. I did them just perfect. The men, they just weld— boom, they don't care—it was a good weld, but messy. I was very particular."*

THE HUNTSVILLE AND REDSTONE ARSENALS

In 1941, the U.S. Army built two army plants near the town of Huntsville, Alabama. The Huntsville Arsenal was built to make chemical weapons such as mustard gas and tear gas. The Redstone Arsenal produced ammunition such as bombs, shells, and grenades.

At first, women working at the Huntsville and Redstone arsenals were hired to do such work as testing and inspecting parts, while men did the heavy work. However, as more and more men signed up for the war, women began doing more production work. They worked as forklift operators, truck drivers, and tool operators. By the end of 1942, women were doing about 40% of the work on the production lines. By 1943, women-only crews were becoming common. These crews became known for working efficiently and getting work done on schedule.

Top: Women assemble aircraft. Bottom: Women build a bomber.

THE RICHMOND SHIPYARDS

care plans and set up daycare centers where people could leave their children while they were working.

When the war ended in 1945, the Richmond Shipyards closed just as quickly as they had opened. Today, the site of the old shipyards is home to the Rosie the Riveter Memorial Park, built to honor women who worked on the home front during World War II.

Left: The **Robert E. Peary** is launched after being built in the Richmond Shipyards in record time. Once the keel, or foundation, had been laid, it took just four days for the rest of the ship to be built. It usually took two months to build this type of ship.

Below: Henry J. Kaiser climbs up the mast of a ship at the Richmond Shipyards.

The Richmond Shipyards in California built more ships than any other facility in the country, employing thousands of people, many of them skilled female workers. Some were African American women from the rural South who left their homes for the promise of better jobs.

The migration of workers to the Richmond Shipyards had a huge effect on the town of Richmond, where the population increased from 20,000 in 1941 to 100,000 by 1943. Workers lived in tents, boats, and cars as they waited for houses to be built.

A man named Henry J. Kaiser ran the shipyards. He was ahead of his time because he cared about his workers and wanted to make sure they were treated well. He offered medical

African American women played an important part in building ships at the Richmond Shipyards.

4 *After the War*

On May 8, 1945, the U.S. declared victory in Europe, and, on September 2, victory in Japan. The war was finally over. The troops began to return home, and when they did, they needed jobs.

As employers hired returning soldiers, women found themselves being forced out of the workplace. Many of the factories and war production plants closed down altogether, and women, especially African American women, were the first to lose their jobs. In factories that stayed open, women in skilled jobs were often **laid off** and replaced with men with no experience.

Postwar Propaganda: Back to the Kitchen!

During the war, the image of Rosie the Riveter had inspired women to work outside the home. Propaganda after the war encouraged them to excel as homemakers. Women were sent the message that leaving the workforce to make room for the returning troops was the best way to serve their country.

After World War II, the U.S. economy was booming, and families could afford to buy new houses and cars. Factories that once produced war equipment changed over to making products for regular citizens, such as new and better household appliances. Postwar propaganda tried to get women excited about buying those products. In stark contrast to the images of working women seen during the war, postwar advertisements in magazines, in newspapers, and on television showed happy housewives in their modern kitchens, surrounded by gleaming new stoves and refrigerators. Television became popular in the 1950s, and television programs in the 1950s and '60s showed very traditional families with working fathers and stay-at-home mothers.

Women Want to Keep Working

For some women, it was a relief to give up their wartime jobs. They were tired of working long hours and taking care of their homes and families at the same time. But many women who had joined the workforce felt differently. In 1945, polls indicated that as many as 85% of women workers wanted to keep their jobs after the war.

Many newspaper and television commercials showed women as housewives.

Some women needed to keep working simply to support their families. According to Marian Sousa:

> *"There were women who needed to keep their jobs, there were a lot that needed to do that....When you think of people who came from the South, especially black women that were supporting children, they needed to keep their jobs."*

More importantly, however, war work had allowed women to acquire new skills and do jobs that hadn't been open to them before the war. Earning their own money had given them a sense of freedom and independence. Working outside the home, and especially working in skilled jobs, gave women more control over their lives, and many women were reluctant to give that up.

GAINS AND LOSSES

Before the war, in 1940, women made up 24% of the workforce. By the peak of the war in 1944, this figure had risen sharply, to a record 36%. Five years after the end of the war, 30% of workers were women, and by 1960 this figure had risen to 33%. This reveals that, despite the pressure to stay at home, many women did continue to work after the war. In order to keep working, many women were forced to take the same kinds of low-paying, less-skilled jobs they were limited to before the war.

Patricia Buls, draftsperson, recalls:

> *"I was going to see if I could find a job doing secretarial work, and I went to one store, some sort of a manufacturing place, to make an application, and I heard the woman in there say, 'Well, you can't expect us to be paying you the amount of money you made in the shipyards.' She said, 'A hundred and twenty dollars is it. That's the most you'll ever make here.' When I heard that, I got up and left."*

After the war, many women were forced to take lower-paying and less-skilled jobs such as phone operators and office assistants.

During the 1960s, women began campaigning for equality in the workplace. A major step forward was the Civil Rights Act of 1964, which banned discrimination against a person in the workplace because of race or gender. This law gave women the power to fight discrimination in court.

By 1970, 38% of workers were women, and since then, the number has increased steadily. In 2006, 46%, or almost half, of all workers were women.

ROSIE'S LEGACY

Even today, there is inequality in the workplace. Women still encounter discrimination and sometimes have to fight for the same pay and opportunities men receive. But thanks to the huge strides taken by American women during World War II, women today have far more choices than ever before about how to live their lives. This is the lasting legacy of Rosie the Riveter and the millions of women she represented.

> *"Nowadays things have changed and women are equal, even if they're still not getting the same pay in some things. If I were still a draftsman, I would expect to get the same pay as those who were trained the same. That's only right."*
>
> — Marian Sousa, draftsperson

A Comparison of Women's Earnings to Men's Earnings

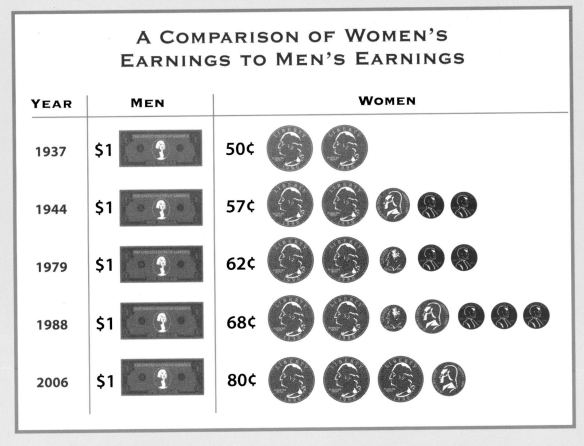

Year	Men	Women
1937	$1	50¢
1944	$1	57¢
1979	$1	62¢
1988	$1	68¢
2006	$1	80¢

Even today, for every dollar a man makes, a woman makes less.

APPENDIX: TIMELINE OF MAJOR EVENTS

September 1939	World War II breaks out in Europe.
December 7, 1941	Japanese planes attack Pearl Harbor.
December 8, 1941	The U.S. declares war on Japan.
December 11, 1941	The U.S. declares war on Germany and Italy.
1942	Rosie the Riveter first appears on a poster with the slogan "We Can Do It!"
March 1943	Rosie the Riveter is featured on the front page of *The Saturday Evening Post*.
May 8, 1945	The U.S. declares victory in Europe.
September 2, 1945	The U.S. declares victory in Japan; World War II ends.
July 1964	The Civil Rights Act prohibits discrimination on the grounds of race or gender.
1997	The real Rosie the Riveter, Rose Will Monroe, dies at age 77.

GLOSSARY

arsenal: all the weapons and equipment that a country has

chaperone: a person who watches over the safety of others

competent: capable or adequate

civilian: a person who isn't in the armed forces or the police force

discrimination: the unfair treatment of people because of their race, gender, or age

distorted: misleading or false

evacuate: to take someone from a dangerous place to safety

home front: the population and activities of a country that is at war

impoverished: poor

laid off: when someone has lost his or her job

perseverance: determination

promoting: advertising or encouraging people to support something

propaganda: information that is spread to influence others

rationing: a controlled distribution of goods

recruit: a new member of an armed force

riveter: a person whose job is to bolt pieces of metal together

strike: when many workers refuse to work to prove a point

supervisor: a person who manages other workers

theater of war: an area where a war is being fought

union: an organization of employees formed to bargain with the employer

welder: a person who joins together metal pieces or parts using heat

BIBLIOGRAPHY

Books

Adams, Simon. *20th Century, A Visual History*. Dorling Kindersley Limited, London, 1996.

Seager, Joni. *The State of Women in the World Atlas* (Penguin, 1977), cited in MacDonald, Fiona. *Equal Opportunities*, Belitha Press, 2002.

Websites

Bureau of Labor Statistics, www.bls.gov

Quotes from Marian Sousa, Altha Humphrey, Phyllis Gould, Matilda Foster, Polly Russell, Patricia Buls, and Harriete Stewart from oral history transcripts at: bancroft.berkeley. edu/ROHO/projects/rosie/

Teacher Oz's Kingdom of History–20th and 21st Century America. Internet.
Database available online. www.teacheroz.com/20thcent.htm
Dates accessed March 24, 2007–April 28, 2007

Teacher Oz's Kingdom of History–U.S. Government. Internet.
Database available online. www.teacheroz.com/government.htm
Dates accessed March 24, 2007–April 28, 2007

Teacher Oz's Kingdom of History–Women's History and Impact on the World. Internet.
Database available online. www.teacheroz.com/women.htm
Dates accessed March 24, 2007–April 28, 2007

Teacher Oz's Kingdom of History–World War II. Internet.
Database available online. www.teacheroz.com/wwii.htm
Dates accessed March 24, 2007–April 28, 2007

Useful site for images relating to women working during WW II: www.loc.gov/rr/print/list/ 126_rosi.html

U.S. Department of Defense, www.defenselink.mil

U.S. Department of Labor, www.dol.gov

U.S. Library of Congress, www.loc.gov

Wikipedia, www.wikipedia.org

Women During World War II, 1999 Women in America. Woodbridge, Conn.: Primary Source Microfilm. Student Resource Center–College Edition

Women Working in World War II, 1941. Discovering U.S. History. Online Detroit: Gale, 2003. Student Resource Center–College Edition

INDEX